CHANGED HEARTS

OTHER BOOKS BY
CHARLES COLSON

CHANGED HEARTS

THE SOLUTION
TO AMERICA'S CRIME PROBLEM

**STORIES FROM
THE MINISTRY FOUNDED BY**

CHARLES COLSON

PRISON FELLOWSHIP MINISTRIES
P.O. Box 17500, Washington, DC 20041

Prison Fellowship is a fellowship of men and women who, motivated by their love for the Lord Jesus Christ and in obedience to His commands, have joined together to exhort and assist His church in the prisons and in the community in its ministries to prisoners, ex-prisoners, and their families, and to promote biblical standards of justice in the criminal justice system.

All photos by David Singer except for p. 15, Anne Rood; p. 21, Alice Lawson Cox; p. 57, Dean Ridings.

Printed in the United States of America.

93 92 91 90 89 4 3 2 1

CONTENTS

FOREWORD

Crime is one of the biggest, and certainly most frightening, problems facing Americans today. Newspaper headlines keep both the terrifying stories of crime and its victims and the corresponding crisis in our prisons in the forefront of most people's minds. Meanwhile experts are throwing up their hands in frustration. Prisons don't cure crime. Nothing seems able to stem this crisis.

But those of us who have the privilege to be involved in Prison Fellowship's ministry have seen far different stories than those that flood the six o'clock news. They are the stories of changed lives, of men and women once caught in a cycle of crime, distrust, and alienation now restored, living responsible lives and serving others as part of the Body of Christ.

That's what this book is all about. It includes just a few of the thousands of stories of prisoners Prison Fellowship has touched, whose lives have been transformed forever by Christ, and just a few of the hundreds of stories we've featured in Prison Fellowship's monthly newsletter, *Jubilee*, over the years.

In the pages that follow you'll read about Willie Rios, a former drug addict who came to a strong and joyous faith in Jesus Christ. Willie's past drug use resulted in AIDS, however—and in his final days, even as his body wasted away, he was a vigorous testimony to Christ's power to change lives.

You'll read about George Taylor, a tall man with a deep, rich voice. George served time in prison, got involved with Prison Fellowship seminars, and is now one of the most well-beloved chaplains the prison system has ever known.

You'll read the heartwarming—and sometimes heart-breaking—stories of inmates' children and what God has done through His people to bring them hope and joy at Christmastime.

Each of these stories is unique. But they are bound by the common thread of the love and miraculous power of Jesus Christ, who can take any life and utterly transform it. And each of these lives is touching the lives of others. This is what C. S. Lewis called "the good infection" that passes from one person to the next. This is what changes society at large.

These are stories of hope, of humor, of struggles. Prisons are hard and stony places; and yet those whose hearts are softened by God have found them a fertile mission field that has yielded rich fruit.

In a day when institutions institute failure and huge social problems like crime seem hopelessly intractable, when frustration is widespread, there is hope. That hope is in the power of God—God relentlessly changing individual lives, one by one. I hope you will be touched as you read. May God bless you.

—Charles W. Colson

Washington, D.C.

1

JOHN & DARLENE BERRY

JOHN BERRY: A NEW CREATION

It's Tuesday, a typical sweltering summer day in Oklahoma City. John Berry, the new-car sales manager, leaves his office, takes off his suit coat, and walks through the maze of dazzling new models at Joe Coker Pontiac-GMC. As the robust, 42-year old black man exits the showroom, he beams as if he's taking the afternoon off after closing an expensive fleet deal.

John, a portrait of success, jumps into his small pickup truck, loosens his tie, and heads not for the golf course or the spa but for his regular appointment at John H. Lilley Correctional Center in Boley, Oklahoma. At a Bible study there he'll tell prisoners about Jesus' life-changing power. John speaks from experience: He's served hard time for armed robbery.

As John drives through the Oklahoma City streets, his mind fills with memories. The third of 10 children, John grew up in an Oklahoma City suburb. His father, who would wander in and out of his family's lives, lived on the streets. The demands of child rearing fell to "Mama."

John feigned the Christian belief taught by his mother, but felt drawn instead to the more appealing message preached by the lifestyle of his dad, a drinker and ladies' man. In 1965, as a young navy recruit, John married a striking teenager named

Darlene and began to follow his father's example.

But it was drugs rather than alcohol that captured the young man's attention. At his first duty station in the navy, John started to smoke marijuana. "It came to the point where it didn't do the job," recalls John. "I was always looking to repeat that first experience, but I couldn't. And that led to other drugs—acid, heroin, cocaine—you name it."

In 1968, John was honorably discharged from the navy. Back in Oklahoma, he found that Darlene had become a Christian at a revival and had begun to take their young son to church—along with John's mother. Darlene challenged her husband's hypocritical claim to Christian faith.

"Darlene was right," says John. "I knew about Jesus, but I hadn't given Him my life; the Lord wasn't in my heart. The drugs, the women—it was just a terrible, terrible life I was living."

During the next few years, John tried to quit his drug habit and work a respectable job. He took a position as assistant manager of a convenience market, and the Berrys had two more children. "But before long it was back to the drug scene, and back to the women," says John. "A little bit of sin leads to a lot of it . . . I was a fool."

John started to spend more time away from home and with three other black men from the streets. "I let the peer pressure get through," says John. "I wanted to be big—to wear nice clothes, drive big cars, have nice jewelry—and not work. So I started getting into little things, like burglary, and really got into cocaine."

One morning in 1975, John and his friends were "ripped" on drugs when they robbed a savings and loan. The small band got away with $60,000.

John laid low after that, cutting down on drugs and getting a job selling custom vans. But he continued to stay away from home. "I didn't think about my family," John says about his years on the streets. "It was *me. John.* I had to take care of *myself,* and I figured everything else would take care of itself.''

Even though John would stay away for long periods of time, Darlene would try to entice him to stay home by making meals and buying gifts for him when he was home. Although her faith in God would sometimes waver, Darlene gained strength in prayer—strength she'd need for the tough days ahead.

A year after the bank robbery, John was called out of a sales meeting—and arrested. Eventually he was convicted, serving three-and-a-half years of a seven-year prison sentence. Darlene stood by her husband. "My father died when I was in the seventh grade," says Darlene. "I was very close to him. I was also close to my brother Donnell, who was murdered. So I had this fear that those I loved the most would be taken away from me. And I didn't want to lose John, too."

Yet John took her faithfulness for granted. "I thought I was the one going through this," he says. "I was angry, frustrated. I didn't think about what my family was feeling: The regular visits Darlene made, the old jalopy she was driving, the three kids she was raising out there by herself." As he prepared for release in 1979, John told Darlene he would never change, he would end up in prison time and again, that she'd be better off without him. John wanted out, and Darlene granted him a divorce.

"Prison did nothing to rehabilitate me," says John. "And I needed help!" After his release, John returned to auto sales— and drugs. He had everything he'd wanted: freedom from family responsibilities, money to spend, yet he was so empty. He tried to fill the emptiness—to escape reality—with drugs.

Then, late one night in September 1982, John pulled his new sedan into a vacant lot. It was one of the rare times he wasn't on drugs in those days, but even so, he stumbled from the car. In desperation, John fell to his knees and wept. As he did, he heard his mother's words from long ago: "Cast all your burdens upon the Lord, Johnny. Give Him your life . . . " He'd spent his whole life in search of personal pleasure, and now felt so hollow. "Jesus, I need You!" he cried bitterly. "If You want my life, take it!"

But when he considered what he'd have to give up, he added, "I can't do it . . . " Within the hour, John had met up with a friend who had some "good stuff." When he left his friend's apartment, head spinning, John raced off into the Oklahoma City night. When he came to his senses, he was in jail: He'd wrapped his car around a telephone pole.

In jail, his experience in the vacant lot started to sink in. "God began to work on me deep within," John says. "He told me, 'You've got to give your life to Me if you want Me to have it. You said you needed Me! So what are you going to do now?' " After three days, John was out on bail and pending trial. He agreed to attend church with his mother and Darlene. There he listened attentively to the salvation message.

"The next thing I knew I was at the altar," says John. "I told the pastor, 'I want the Lord to take charge of my life.' I admitted that I was guilty—not my wife, my mom, my peer group, the world, but *me*—I was wrong, and that I wanted the Lord to come into my heart. My life has taken a 100 percent turn since then."

John and Darlene rekindled their friendship over the next several months. They often prayed—for each other—and shared favorite Bible passages together. Before his trial in May 1983, John asked Darlene to remarry him; she accepted. At the wedding, John presented the Gospel message, and one man, moved to tears, received Christ.

Although the prospects of a Christian marriage excited the couple, John's trial loomed heavily on their hearts. "I began to pray for John's will to be done," says John, "and not God's will. When I stood in front of the judge that day in court and he said, 'Two years,' I said, 'Lord, where are You?' " His pastor stepped up to him and said, "John, the Lord wants to use you. I want you to go back and learn as much as you can—study the Word of God." John did just that.

One day, while Darlene was visiting John, she noticed a poster advertising an upcoming Prison Fellowship seminar at the facility. The Berrys attended the In-Prison Seminar, conducted by Herman Heade, a one-time bank robber turned minister.

"Darlene and I led a small group at the seminar," says John. "I still remember its name: God's Laborers for the Harvest. That's when the Lord pressed it that He wanted me in prison ministry. The day I got out (of prison) I got in touch with Prison Fellowship."

Today John leads two prison Bible studies, coordinates local volunteers, and Darlene leads a Bible study at a women's prison. Together, they participate in other Prison Fellowship programs, head the evangelistic committee at their church, Tabernacle Baptist, and help to spark interest in prison ministry at other churches in the black community.

Now, as he ministers in prisons and in his community, John is astutely aware of people like his old self. "If I see someone like the old me—and I sometimes do—I *pray* for him," says John. "I know the old John—I'm not that man anymore. He's dead. It's Christ who lives in me now: 'If anyone is in Christ, he is a new creation; the old has gone, the new has come!' That's me!"

—*Dean Ridings*

2

AL & NADINE PETERS

A NEBRASKA FARM FAMILY STICKS BY EX·PRISONERS

The large bulletin board on the wall of Al and Nadine Peters's old farmhouse near Hampton, Nebraska, overflows with snapshots and family portraits—they are the snug kitchen's focal point.

But as Nadine proudly points out each photo and tells the stories behind them, you soon realize that the people in the photos aren't just friends and family. Many are ex-prisoners from the nearby Nebraska Center for Women (NCW)—but that's just like saying "family" to Al and Nadine, two of Prison Fellowship's most active volunteers.

For 11 years, the Peterses have faithfully served at this prison in York about 15 miles from their home, if you take the back dirt roads around the surrounding farms. They lead a weekly Prison Fellowship Bible study, but their ministry includes much more. You can tell from their phone bill and the way they plan vacations. Trips for this fourth-generation farmer and his wife don't always take them to the mountains or warmer climates, but to the homes of former NCW inmates. As Al says: "If we care about them in prison, we have to care about them on the outside."

Such caring follow-up brought the Peterses the Ex-Prisoner Ministry Award during the Prison Fellowship National Volunteer Conference last March near the ministry's headquarters in Reston, Virginia. Speaking at the conference, Al cited two Scriptures that underscore their ministry. Paraphrasing Luke 6:32–33, he said, "We have to love differently than the world loves" and from 2 Timothy 1:4: "Recalling your tears, I long to see you again."

The Peterses' ministry to prisoners began in 1974 when they taught a young adult Sunday school class at their church. When they reached James's discussion of the relationship between faith and deeds, many in the class asked, "We need to share our faith. Where can we go?"

"I had been to the prison several times with a women's group from church," Nadine says. "I suggested that, and it took hold."

Once a month for four years, about 15 class members met at the prison for softball and fellowship with the inmates. When the class ended, Al and Nadine continued visiting the women and began a Bible study at the prison.

The tragedy of their young son's death 18 years ago has helped the Peterses identify with the inmates. "Gregg's death prepared us to minister to the hurting," Al says. "We can weep with those who weep and rejoice with those who rejoice."

Al's infectious, jovial manner balanced by Nadine's more quiet, discerning spirit draws each woman into the circle. They also model a Christian marriage for the women, many of whom have known only fractured relationships. Three years ago, they brought cake to the Bible study to celebrate their twenty-third wedding anniversary with the women. "We want them to know stable relationships are possible in Christ," Nadine says.

The Peterses lived in Chicago after their marriage in 1959 while Al worked with an inner-city ministry. After two years there, the business of the family farm brought them back to Nebraska, though Al felt full-time ministry might be his calling. "But the Lord led in a different way," he says, "and gave us a ministry all the same."

Their 500-acre farm has been in the Peters family for more than 100 years—since Al's great-grandfather bought the land from the Union Pacific Railroad. On this rolling, rich land in south-central Nebraska, the Peterses raise corn and soybeans. Each winter, as the land lies dormant, they take an extended vacation. Last February, before coming to Washington for Prison Fellowship's volunteer conference, they visited their two older daughters in Wichita, Kansas, then drove on to Texas, Florida, and Kentucky to see former inmates, one who has been out eight years.

One of the most obvious fruits of the Peterses' ministry is the new stone chapel facing the prison courtyard—a much-needed place of worship that has brought new vitality and interest to the Christian programs at the prison.

Since 1981, Nadine has been chairman of the NCW chapel fund drive. The project began in 1977 when an inmate wrote a letter to the editor of the Omaha newspaper complaining that the women at NCW had no place to worship God.

Housewife Carroll Falk from Albion, an hour's drive from York, read the letter and suggested it as a project to the local Christian Women United Club. The club promptly sent in the first $50 to help build a chapel.

Despite the tough times economically for Nebraskan farmers, thousands across the state gave generously. In seven years, the committee raised more than $100,000; a quarter of it from members of Al and Nadine's church in Henderson.

Mrs. Falk, along with Chuck Colson and hundreds of supporters, attended the chapel dedication in May. She said, "It was amazing to see what had happened just because of a simple letter." This echoed Chuck's message that God most often works not through the powerful, but the powerless. Because one inmate expressed concern in a letter, and a woman responded, the heads and hearts of the people of Nebraska turned toward this tiny prison.

Now the Bible studies and In-Prison Seminars are held in

the 2,000 square-foot chapel instead of a 20-by-20-foot visitors room, where speakers fought to be heard over the humming soft-drink machines.

So, when long-time Prison Fellowship instructor Jane Douglass White comes to teach the first In-Prison Seminar in the new chapel this month, she will be pleasantly surprised by her new surroundings. She'll also be pleased to see NCW's newest volunteer, Sherry Knopick.

Two-and-a-half years ago, 21-year-old Sherry, then an inmate, stood during the last session of a seminar at NCW. Wiping away a tear, she said, "All my life I've been chasing men. Last night I met the man who fulfills all my needs—Jesus Christ."

After her release, Sherry became reacquainted with Paul Knopick, a young man she knew while in high school. Paul says, "I knew once Sherry got her life straightened out, she was the woman I wanted to marry." He had made a commitment to Christ about the same time as Sherry.

Now married, the Knopicks join Al and Nadine in the prison for the Bible study. "The women encourage me, but it works both ways," Sherry says, "because they see how I've changed."

For Al and Nadine, the blessing is seeing Sherry happily married and returning to prison with her husband. "It's a beautiful thing to see a woman we've worked with come full circle," Al says.

And when a woman in the Bible study is released, she sees perhaps for the first time the extent of the Peterses' concern. Leaving NCW is a time of happiness, relief, and also of uncertainty. But of one thing they are certain—Al and Nadine's friendship. Before any woman walks out the gate, the Peterses write their address and phone number in the front of her Bible. They are never far away.

—Anne Rood

3

DARWIN COON *(left)* **& DAVID WOOLRIDGE**

AN EX·PRISONER FROM ALCATRAZ STOPS RUNNING

"Alcatraz never was no good for anybody."—The last prisoner to leave San Francisco Bay's famed maximum-security prison upon its closing in 1963.

The blue lights of a highway patrol car set Darwin Coon's heart racing. Not knowing it was a routine check, he jammed the accelerator while his partner whipped out a .45 automatic and opened fire. The two men, recently escaped from Nevada State Prison and fresh from their fifth bank robbery, didn't want to answer questions. As the patrol car roared after them, Darwin, 25, flung open the door of his '57 Chevy and ran into the streets of Sioux City, Iowa. He was agile, despite the $16,000 stuffed in his shirt and two pistols shoved into his belt. Spying a manhole cover, he lifted the lid, shimmied in, and descended into the darkness of the city's storm sewer system. He was home—where he had played as a kid—but the game was over the next day when he was caught 40 miles outside of town.

Darwin had learned the art of escaping early in life. When he was 10, his parents had split up, and the sandy-haired, brown-eyed boy had moved to Sioux City with his dad and sister. His father had worked nights and slept days, so Darwin had been left to his own devices. Finding school no challenge to his quick mind, he'd often escaped to the river with a fishing pole. But that trick had been called to a halt when he was 13 and the state sent him to Eldora Training School for Boys because of truancy.

In theory Eldora was run by two houseparents, but in truth it had been ruled by the school's toughest kids—a "captain" and "lieutenant"—who nightly beat up those who misbehaved. Wanting to avoid regular work detail, Darwin had set out to earn a reputation as the meanest kid. Soon he was captain, learning how to steal and beat the law. In fact, Eldora had trained Darwin so well that he spent 25 of the next 27 years in institutions.

The first years in and out of reformatories had been a game—trying to be the toughest when "inside," to lay his hands on the most money when out. "I thought," says Darwin, now 55, "if I had money, I could do anything—really live it up." Drinking, gambling, chasing women, owning nice clothes, and driving fast cars had lured him. Prison walls and bank safes had only challenged him. That is, until Leavenworth—where he was sent after escaping Nevada State Prison and robbing the bank in Iowa.

At Leavenworth he was told that if he messed up once, he'd be sent to Alcatraz, the end of the line. So at the penitentiary, the game was to help others escape. Five months after Darwin's arrival, authorities traced the tools used in a foiled escape attempt to Darwin's work area. Although he was thrown in the "hole" and roughed up daily in an attempt to elicit a confession, the bloodied man refused to admit his part. He'd learned too much at Eldora about intimidating and controlling others; though he was afraid of the prison guards, he defied them. "They may *kill* you," he says today, "but they can't *change* you unless you want to change."

On his twenty-ninth day of solitary, the guards won: At midnight they threw the light on in his cell, ordered him to take a shower, and shackled him. Sleepy-eyed Darwin was bound for Alcatraz.

Suddenly, the game got serious. Riding on the ferry to the desolate 12-acre island off San Francisco and smelling the damp

sea air, Darwin thought, *What have I got myself into?* "It was
the scaredest I've been in my life," he says, recalling the in-
famous prison where he spent four years. "I was 26 years old,
looking at an 80-year sentence in a place where you have to
serve a third of your time before they'll even *consider* parole."

But it was another year before the full consequences hit
him: He had failed at everything—even being a criminal; for
a prisoner, Alcatraz *was* the end of the line.

This realization startled Darwin into action. He stopped
dreaming of ways to escape the pelican-and-prisoner island;
instead he began requesting books on bank robbery trials.
Poring over the cases, he looked for a loophole in his own.

Eventually, Darwin's sleuth work paid off, and by the time
Alcatraz was closed in 1963, he was scheduled for a retrial—
from which he received a new sentence of 20 years. As he joined
the last boatful of prisoners to leave the island, he determined
that he'd stay out of trouble once back at Leavenworth.

There, others knew he was impermeable, but they didn't
know he was praying every night. His mother had become a
Christian, and, when she visited, she encouraged him to call
upon God. In the darkness of his cell he talked to God about
the struggle to stay alive; he asked for help not to go crazy under
the pressure or to give in to rampant homosexuality.

When Darwin was released from prison in 1972, he faced
new fears. He'd once bragged about his escapes, but now he
had to cover them up. When filling out job applications, the
40-year-old wrote that he was a self-employed farmer from
Iowa. The lies worked—Darwin got a job as a maintenance man
in California—but he paid a high price for his deceit. He drank
more and more alcohol to escape from himself.

After nine years on the West Coast, Darwin returned to
Sioux City, where he tended bar—and tried to quench his thirst
for alcohol. "I drank," he says, "because I had to lie so much.
I would drink rather than talk."

Marriage to Marjorie, a frequent patron of the bar where

he worked, didn't cure his addiction as he thought it might. His half-gallon-a-day habit left him continuously sick, until the summer of 1984, when Darwin finally listened to his wife and committed himself to a drug-and-alcohol-abuse center.

While there, he became convinced that God was the "higher power" to which Alcoholics Anonymous referred. Darwin resumed his bedtime prayers and talked with Marge about finding a church in Sioux City. "There was something lacking in my life," he says, "and I hoped church would be the answer."

But seven months after "treatment," still unchurched, he went on a drinking binge. In desperation, Marge called David Woolridge, a man who had gone through detoxification with Darwin. When Darwin sobered up, David suggested that the Coons come to church with him and his wife.

The following Sunday, on a snowy day in January 1985, Darwin and Marge showed up at Victory Chapel in South Sioux City, Nebraska, and there Darwin discovered he could quit running. "Since the day I walked into church, I've never walked into a bar," says Darwin, who with Marge was baptized. Now he serves on the board of deacons. "My mother prayed for me for 40 years. I think the Lord looked out for me all those years in prison because she was praying for me."

It was at Victory Chapel that Darwin first met Bill Everitt, a former bank robber who was working for Teen Challenge in Des Moines and teaching occasional Prison Fellowship seminars. After Bill shared his testimony with the congregation, Darwin pulled him over to the side "You're awfully brave," he said, looking around the room.

"What do you mean?" asked Bill.

"You know," said Darwin, tilting his head, "telling everyone you were a bank robber."

"That was before I was saved," said Bill with a smile. "A lot has happened since then."

Darwin glanced about again. "I was one, too," he

whispered, "but I'm so ashamed, only my wife and pastor know." Then, feeling a new freedom, he told Bill his story.

Two weeks later, at Bill's prompting, Darwin stood before 80 In-Prison Seminar participants at The Men's Reformatory in Anamosa, Iowa. Although his stomach had tensed as the gates clanged shut behind him, God gave him courage. *Can I express myself to all these inmates?* he wondered, but Bill's nod encouraged him. The instructor's words rang in Darwin's ears: "Just tell them."

So Darwin broke his silence and shared the past he had tried to escape. As his tears spilled, he could see Bill's reassuring smile. Afterward he thought, *I hope I got through to somebody, so somebody won't have to go through what I did.* Hearing "Thank you, Jesus" over the applause told him he had.

In the year-and-a-half since then, Darwin has spoken at several Prison Fellowship presentations in churches and prisons throughout Iowa and South Dakota. He has helped start a Philemon Fellowship ex-offender support group and makes monthly visits to Springfield Correctional Center, 90 miles away. "The guys in the joint have been down to the bottom," he says. "They know that you know, so they listen to you. I figure if they rub elbows with Christians long enough, it's bound to rub off."

One person Christianity has rubbed off on is Rhett, a young inmate who committed his life to Jesus at Prison Fellowship's first In-Prison Seminar in Springfield. The former drug dealer began writing Darwin and talking with him at Prison Fellowship's monthly Bible study. Hearing about Darwin's crime-ridden past, Rhett said, "If God can forgive you, I know he can forgive me."

Reflecting on the "wasted" years which God is redeeming, Darwin says, "I used to have to escape everything; now with Jesus I'm home. He's the true end of the line."

—*Alice Lawson Cox*

4

PRAYER, PACKAGES, AND THE PRESENCE OF CHRIST

Christmas had become just a buying experience," says Bob Riera, a commander in the U.S. Navy, "so three years ago our family prayed for a project to help the kids understand that Christmas is not about getting, but giving. When my sister, a Prison Fellowship pen pal, told us about Project Angel Tree, we knew it was the answer."

That year Bob and his wife, Cindy, went to a church in the Virginia suburbs of Washington, D.C. to select a paper angel ornament hung on a specially decorated tree. On the angel, church volunteers had recorded three Christmas-gift wishes for the child of an inmate at Lorton Reformatory, a nearby prison complex. The Rieras and their two children spent a Saturday shopping for just the right presents, and long after returning the gifts to the church, the Rieras prayed for their adopted "angel." They were hooked on Angel Tree.

The following year, Bob and Cindy got their own church involved in the project. Then, in 1987, members of Immanuel Bible Church—primarily white—in Springfield, Virginia, bought presents for more than 100 children of prisoners and sponsored a gift-giving party at the mostly black Allen Chapel A.M.E. Church in the heart of D.C.

The two churches, now in their second year of partnership, are together tackling a year-round ministry to prisoners and their families; Immanuel's resources—clothing, food, and money—reinforce Allen's inner-city savvy and people-power.

The selfless spirit of giving that motivates the Rieras' Angel Tree efforts is spreading across the country. Throughout the year Prison Fellowship has heard reports from coast to coast of inmates' children who have been touched by Angel Tree. Long after the presents are gone, the presence of Christ remains.

A Father's Love

Some years ago a father named Jim bought two shiny, state-of-the-art, 10-speed bicycles: one for his son, Jay, the other for his daughter, Sarah. On Christmas morning the children shrieked with excitement when they saw their gifts. They tore through the neighborhood showing off their prized possessions. Jay soon wore the wheels off his; Sarah, more gentle, took great pride in caring for her special present.

But the family scene soon changed. In 1983, Sarah was killed in a car accident. The house grew quiet, and the grieving family disposed of most of her things. They offered the bike to a cousin—who never came to pick it up. Jim tried to sell it at a garage sale, but no one bought it. The bike stayed in the garage, gathering dust.

Then, in fall 1987, an inmate at Mississippi's Parchman prison filled out an Angel Tree application for his daughter Ginger (not her real name). Though she had had to make do all her life, Ginger had always dreamed big. She didn't know that you weren't supposed to ask for 10-speed bicycles on Angel Tree request forms. But she had wanted one for as long as she could remember.

It was Sunday noon a few weeks before Christmas at the Highland Methodist Church in Meridian, Mississippi. In the service the church's Angel Tree had been explained, and now people were eagerly clustered around the tree at the front of the sanctuary. Though he was caught in conversation, Jim kept his eyes on the tree. The angels were disappearing rapidly.

When Jim finally disengaged himself and rushed to the tree, there was just one angel left. The girl's name was Ginger, and she wanted a 10-speed bike.

That afternoon Jim wheeled Sarah's bike out of the garage. It needed adjustments, a few new parts, and a good cleaning. With great care Jim overhauled the bike, rewrapped the handlebars, rubbed the chrome with a soft, clean rag until it shone, and proudly took the bike back over to the church. When he realized he hadn't checked the brakes, Jim hopped on the bike and took it on a swing through the parking lot, grinning all the way.

When other church volunteers took the gleaming bike to Ginger on Christmas Eve, her face broke into a huge smile as well. The dream gift her dad couldn't deliver was hers—given by another dad who knew what it meant to lose a daughter he loved.

With God There Are No Wrong Addresses

About 700 miles north of Meridian, Jim and Jane Fizzell coordinate Angel Tree projects for the entire city of Chicago, last year providing gifts for more than 3,100 children.

Their dedicated cast of volunteers included a group of teenagers from a suburban church—who delivered gifts several days before Christmas. When the door of one old apartment in a broken down housing project opened to them, a group of children stared in wonder and delight. All these packages—for them? But when the mother came to the door, the teens soon realized they were at the wrong apartment.

Full of apologies, the young volunteers left and delivered the gifts to the right apartment. But the tearful faces of those first children still haunted them. Could they just walk away leaving such dashed hopes? No.

Once the teens got out on the street, they pooled their pocket money and headed for a department store.

Stepping into the foyer out of the Chicago wind, they stopped for a quick prayer. As they finished and raised their heads, they saw an older man from their church watching them. "What are you doing?" he asked. They explained about the wrong address and the disappointed children.

"Come with me," he said, and the teenagers followed him to his office. None of them had known that he was the store manager. He wrote out a store certificate, and set them loose. With armloads of gifts, they returned to the apartment and knocked on the door.

The Cupboard Was Bare

In another part of Chicago's inner city, an inmate's family had but one Angel Tree request for all the children: thermal underwear. The mother lived on the top floor of the Robert Taylor homes, a high-rise project housing 25,000 people. A notorious crime and drug area, its elevators had been broken by gang members trying to force people to use the stairwells, where they could be easily mugged.

The PF suburban volunteer who offered to deliver the gifts to this family prayed for the Lord's protection as he walked up to the apartment. When the door opened, he gasped. The room was bare: no carpet, no bed, no furniture, no food. Not even enough clothes for the children. As he handed each child a wrapped package of thermal underwear, he was overcome with the need before him. "I'll be back," he said.

And he kept his word. He returned with other church members, bearing a huge food basket, some clothing, and a few pieces of furniture. The volunteers have been back since then, continuing to furnish a barren home with hope and love.

Not Just Giving, but Sharing

Last Christmas the spirit of giving also thrived in the Dallas area, where the Valley View Christian Church sponsored 150 "angels." One family that volunteered to take gifts to an inmate's family arrived at the home on Christmas Eve. Even though the givers had known that Christmas would likely be dismal for this needy family, it wasn't until they walked inside that they began to feel the loneliness and isolation faced by the inmate's family.

There was no Christmas tree, no cards from friends, no festive music or sense of celebration. As they talked with the mother, they also realized there was very little food.

As the volunteers drove back home, they were welcomed by Christmas tree lights and all the warmth they represent. They felt good about delivering the gifts, but leaving the presents and retreating back to their own secure haven didn't seem quite fair: Was there more they could give?

On Christmas morning the family woke up early, opened their gifts to one another, then dismantled the carefully trimmed tree. They wrapped their Christmas dinner in aluminum foil and loaded it into the car. Then they packed the tree lights and decorations as well, tied the tree into the trunk, and set off for the inmate's home.

As they pulled up in front of the house, they could see the inmate's children at the window, their eyes wide at the sight of the loaded car and the careening Christmas tree. The volunteer family jumped out. "Merry Christmas!" they shouted.

The door opened and Christ came in.

—Ellen Santilli Vaughn and Alice Lawson Cox
with special thanks to Rita Wells

5

GEORGE TAYLOR WITH INMATE

A PRISON CHAPLAIN MODELS CHRIST'S COMPASSION

The stand-off between 1,300 inmates corralled in Lorton's prison yard and the hundreds of correctional officers and police who surrounded them was entering its third night. Fires lit by inmates had reduced overcrowded prison dorms at Washington, D.C.'s, central prison facility to charred, smoldering shells. The inmates had gone without food for more than 24 hours, and each attempt to bring them water ignited new violence.

Suddenly, in the cold glare of spotlights, a lone silhouette stood in the no-man's land that separated the opposing groups. For a second night, one of the wardens had called George Taylor, chaplain from neighboring Youth Center I, for help.

The night before, George had waded into the suffocating summer heat with a vague desire to somehow relieve the explosive tension among the huddled, frightened captives. "Once out there, I thought, *What in the world am I doing here?*" remembers the tall emissary. "Just then a brother stopped me and said, 'Hey Reverend, pray for us.' "

As George began to pray, 150 inmates—many Christians, others just scared and seeking security in a group—clasped hands in a huge circle and joined him in his petition for God's mercy. "I went out to encourage the brothers that everything would be all right, that they weren't alone, that somebody cared," he says.

Now he was in the yard again—this time bringing water to quench thirst and cool tempers. "I told them to get in lines," he says, "and that if they kept things orderly, I'd bring them all the water they could drink." That statement is an apt metaphor for this ex-offender's ministry.

George thinks of himself as a "junk" man. "I've come off the junk pile," he says in deep, warm tones. "I don't forget from whence I've come, but Somebody laundered me. When you get cleaned up from the inside out, you don't just believe it—you live it."

George decided to "live it" as the result of a Prison Fellowship seminar he attended nine years ago. It was a turning point for him.

Although raised by a devout Christian mother (she was a preacher), George was always dazzled by "things." "I grew up in Detroit already grown," he says. "I was a real entrepreneur and learned to hustle very, very early."

At 16 he was sent to reform school for breaking and entering. "My mother said I was hanging around with the wrong crowd," he says. "But she was wrong: I was part of the crowd." When he was released from Michigan's Ionia State Prison four years later, he determined to stay out of trouble.

But he also set his sights on becoming a millionaire. He went to Los Angeles, where he used his con skills, engaging style, and glib tongue to slide down the fast lane. "Although I wanted to do the right thing, I also didn't want to be a have-not. I wanted to be a have," he explains.

He graduated from Elizabeth Bible College, then attended Fuller Theological Seminary, and was ordained. "But I still wasn't totally committed," he says. "I wore the label 'Christian' just like a lot of folks. I don't question what a person says he is, but you have to look at his lifestyle—can you see a clear-cut value system? Coming to the Lord is a shedding-off process. Sometimes being 'born again' takes a long pregnancy. We can love the Lord, but does He come first?''

George pastored a small Missionary Baptist Church whose membership quickly grew to more than 800. He says, ''The Lord really blessed, although at the time I took some credit. I pictured myself as a Martin Luther King and Malcolm X combined. I thought that if my people had more economic clout, they would be a little more spiritual.''

At the same time, George passionately pursued his million-dollar dream through banking and real estate schemes. ''I put a couple of deals together,'' he says. ''One was seven figures. Our merger and acquisition firm used the liquidity of one bank to buy another. I was going to come away with a million plus. It was 'Taylor' made.'' The federal authorities arrested him.

During his incarceration, George transferred from prison to prison much like Israel wandering in the wilderness. He landed at the federal penitentiary in Terre Haute, Indiana, where chaplain Jim Forsythe would lead him to the promised land. He began by giving George chaplaincy duties in the prison farm camp.

Forsythe then arranged for George to attend a Prison Fellowship Washington Discipleship Seminar. One evening at the seminar, George and Chuck Colson took a walk. ''There were three of us: Chuck, me, and the Holy Spirit,'' he says. For the first time, George saw ''one of the big boys,'' one who could have anything he wanted, give it all up to follow Jesus. As he puts it, ''Chuck set it out the way I'd read about it, but had never seen.''

''After the seminar,'' George says, ''I got my priorities aligned. I came to myself like the Prodigal Son in the pigpen. I came to grips with money. If Chuck could give it up, I could too.'' He finished serving 30 months and was released to a halfway house in hometown Detroit.

There Prison Fellowship State Director Jerry Snyder groomed George to succeed him. ''Jerry put me on his back saying, 'He ain't heavy—he's my brother,'" he says. After serving two years as Michigan state director, George was asked to lead a Prison Fellowship local program.

In September 1985, George left Prison Fellowship's staff to become the D.C. Department of Correction's staff chaplain. The only ex-offender ever employed by the DOC, he now serves as chaplain to two of the prisons in the D.C. prison complex.

George's familiar, fedora-capped form is often seen strolling across the campus, drawing residents like a pied piper. He often stops to pray with groups of inmates, embracing them in his big arms. But most just want to chat; he stops to listen. "If I am to help them," he says, "I must win their respect. I must respect them, too. I tell them that I don't know anybody who doesn't want them except the devil. They epitomize our constant longing for the dignity due God's children."

Assistant Warden Jones says, "The men see him more than any other administrator. Reverend Taylor is here most evenings until nine or ten. He is the stabilizing force in the institution."

George says, "I don't proselytize. I just tell the men what works for me. I can't afford the luxury of giving them bad info. I tell them, 'I can help you clean up, but I'm not going to do it. With the Lord's help, you can do it. You've got to get straight with God's law, then you'll be within the bounds of man's law.' "

In his Bible studies, he gets down in the mired trenches with his men. He feels the cold rain with them. His many caring hugs and handshakes quietly reassure inmates of his passion for his men and his ministry.

—David Singer

6

RICHARD GRAYSON

A VICTIM OF CRIME TURNS HIS ORDEAL INTO DEVOTED SERVICE

At the end of a long, sultry spring day in 1973, an exhausted Richard Grayson reexamined the day's receipts, then tossed a bundle of cash into the safe. Routinely, he set the security alarm of the Claymont, Delaware, Howard Johnson's restaurant, hit the lights, and moved toward the exit. In the dim light, the 27-year-old manager waded through a sea of tables and chairs—ready to accommodate the breakfast crowd, arriving in a few hours.

But suddenly, from out of nowhere, a sawed-off shotgun hit Richard's chest: Two men, with eyes bulging from ski masks, demanded money. "Open the safe!"

Surprise and panic assaulted Richard's body as the intruders spun him around and shoved him toward the office. "I can't *see* to open up the safe," Richard shrieked, as a gruff hand forced him into the dark room. A pistol pressed against his brow. "You can see this, can't you?"

"Hey, the alarm's set," one interrupted. "Let's get out of here!" The two robbers briskly led Richard outside. Jabbing a gun into his waist, threatening his life should he call for help, they sent Richard back in for the money. He obeyed their orders and minutes later emerged with the sack. Quivering, he set it in the vacant street and turned to walk away—just as two police cars sped onto the scene.

"Is everything okay?" a policeman asked, opening the squad car door. Still panic-struck, Richard jumped into the policeman's lap and shouted that he'd just been robbed.

Although the thieves escaped into the darkness, they left behind the bag of money and a Richard Grayson who would never again be the same. Until that night, Richard hadn't given a second thought to the problem of crime or the needs of criminals or victims. Little did he suspect that now, 14 years later, his life would revolve around the criminal justice system.

For years, Richard relived the haunting night a thousand times; he never again closed up the restaurant alone. "You know what fear is when someone's got a gun in your face," he says. "I was terrified after that, always looking over my shoulder."

The uneasiness came to a head about three years after the robbery attempt. In early 1977, not long after the birth of their second child, Richard's wife, Janet, fell into a depression that held on for several years.

"It was a very frustrating time," says Richard, who struggled to understand Janet and to come to grips with the anxiety plaguing his own life. "I didn't know what to do, and I had nowhere to turn." Though Janet's new-found Christian faith didn't restore her to health, as a last resort, Richard asked God to prove His existence by giving him clear direction. "Lord, what am I to do? She's got to get well . . ."

Richard felt at peace when Janet began to receive counsel from a Christian psychologist. And God's answer to Richard's short prayer led to a major commitment: He accepted Jesus Christ as well. The Graysons started to attend church, and Richard began to read the Bible and go to Christian meetings.

At one such gathering, Richard heard Art Linkletter tell about America's drug crisis and his daughter's drug-related death. "Also on the bill was Chuck Colson," says Richard. "At the time, his name wasn't familiar." But Richard left the auditorium with a copy of Colson's autobiography, *Born Again*.

"I was impressed with Chuck's testimony," says Richard. "So I used the reply card in the back to write Prison Fellowship and see what I could do." He began corresponding with several prison pen pals. And when Colson was preparing to head the first Prison Fellowship In-Prison Seminar at the Delaware Correctional Center in the fall of 1979, Richard received a letter from Prison Fellowship asking him to lead small-group discussions.

It wasn't a routine decision. How could his mind not return to the haunting restaurant scene—the masked men, the shotgun in his chest, the threats, the terror? Once again, Richard prayed for God's help to make a key decision. He was convinced that God wanted him to get involved.

At the seminar, Richard quickly befriended Dave, a prisoner in his small group. "We found that we had been at a lot of the same places. He'd gone to the University of Delaware and studied in the business school, and so had I," says Richard. He began to think about what it was that made Dave, a new believer in Christ, so different from himself. "Nothing," Richard says. "We were both sinners saved by God's grace."

After the seminar, Richard began to attend a regular Bible study at the prison and to help men like Dave grow in Christ.

In mid 1985, after discovering Justice Fellowship, the national criminal justice organization associated with Prison Fellowship Ministries, Richard started to concentrate his efforts on the other side of prison walls.

In his years as a volunteer, he'd seen the prison population swell. He'd wondered about alternatives to imprisonment for nonviolent offenders. And he'd wondered if any offenders were being held accountable to restore their victims.

"I was a victim," says Richard. "It's difficult to describe what that means: You have a 'personal space' you invite people into. But when somebody forces himself into that area, you feel like your whole being has been violated. That's how I felt."

Richard says he agrees with Justice Fellowship President

Dan Van Ness's view that it is an injustice that victims are isolated from the criminal justice system almost from the moment the crime is committed. Restitution helps to bring the victim back into the picture, he maintains, and can lead to restoration.

At Justice Fellowship's invitation, Richard joined the year-old Delaware Task Force, which was lobbying the state's Sentencing Accountability Commission (SENTAC) and the legislature to develop alternative punishments that would hold property offenders accountable, while reserving prison space for the most serious offenders.

Investigating the state's criminal justice system, the Delaware Task Force found a crucial flaw. While the state required restitution, many property offenders couldn't afford to pay it. Thus, the sentence was either probation or prison—two extremes on opposite ends of the pole and neither repaying victims. An employment-oriented restitution program was needed, but when the state's Criminal Justice Council sought proposals, no established group came forward to administer it.

In response, a group of task-force members jumped in and proposed Project Repay—a program designed to put offenders to work to repay their victims. Not only was it accepted, but Project Repay received a $24,000 federal victim-assistance grant. Its director, Richard Grayson, had recently left restaurant management and earned a degree in corrections.

"Project Repay gave offenders a second chance," Richard says. "There's a song by a Christian composer called 'Don't Shoot the Wounded.' We often shoot our wounded—society locks offenders up with the attitude 'keep them in prison and let them suffer.' But Project Repay said, 'Do you want a second chance? Then make restitution.' "

In April 1986, Project Repay began providing "hours of work" so offenders could earn money to pay back their victims. Along with many other federally funded programs, the project's funding was discontinued in January 1988. Even though Richard will no longer work for Project Repay, he's committed to his work with people involved with crime. Immediately, he's plunging into a new position—as a New Castle County probation officer.

Meanwhile, the Justice Fellowship Delaware Task Force has completed its work: SENTAC's sentencing-reform bills passed through the legislature, and the task force created and helped to pass a bill that improves the payment of restitution to victims. Justice Fellowship will continue to work for criminal justice reform in Delaware; later this year task-force veterans and dues-paying Justice Fellowship members will be forming a pilot Justice Fellowship Chapter.

In the end, Richard is not concerned with "success" so much as being faithful to the work God has given him: attacking America's prison problem on many fronts. "I don't know if I've had that many successes," he modestly says. "But my whole philosophy is that at the end of my life, if I've helped just one person, that's good enough for me."

This perspective provides Richard with the strength to "keep plugging away"—on both sides of prison walls. "The Lord has led me here," Richard says of his new probation-officer job as well as his prison ministry endeavors. "He's taken care of me to this point . . . So I'll serve Him here."

—*Dean Ridings*

7

LINDA BOWMAN

HOOKED ON HEROIN, HEALED BY LOVE

Seventeen-year-old Linda smoothed the wrinkles on her jeans and walked onto the dance floor. It was her first year in Tidewater Virginia's public schools, and she desperately wanted to be part of the "in" crowd. She danced and drank with her friends until the night's revelry was suddenly interrupted: Someone turned up the lights.

Linda gasped as her father strode into the room and dragged her away. Once home he raged, "If God were to return right now, what would he think?"

Eighteen years later, Linda Bowman still remembers the shame. "I never felt good enough or right enough for my father," recalls the petite brunette, tears in her eyes. "I wanted to feel that I was special to him, but I never felt accepted."

Feelings of inadequacy and unloveliness drove Linda farther from her parents and their God. "The drug culture accepted me where I was," she says. "Taking drugs was an entree into 'the crowd.'"

It was also a means of overcoming her inferiority. Her heroin highs gave her an illusion of omnipotence. By age 24 Linda was living with a pusher and addicted to the hero-making drug he pushed. "It was the only secure life I knew," says Linda. She was soon arrested for selling and distributing heroin. Her world crashed in.

Sitting in the isolation unit at the Virginia Correctional Institution for Women, the frail young woman felt even more unlovable. She had failed everyone. For the first time, Linda realized her helplessness, her inability to escape the mess she had made of her life.

Uncertain whether she would even be heard, Linda asked God for forgiveness. Then she begged Him for even more: *I've got to know your love!*

Wanting to find out for herself who God was, Linda asked a friend to send a Bible she could comprehend. Having never understood the King James Version, she delved into The Living Bible with enthusiasm. "I knew all the judgment and laws," she says, "but I didn't know about His grace and love."

Each time she read one of God's promises, Linda told Him, "Okay, You said this; I'm going to act on it."

In a giant step of faith, she trusted God to help her break free from drugs. Her new life in Christ was so filled with peace that she refused the prison hospital's medicinal drugs, choosing instead to go cold turkey. God honored her trust and set her free from her drug addiction.

Seeing daily evidence of God's love, Linda felt peace in spite of the turmoil that surrounded her in prison. Her incarceration became a time of drawing closer to God. Then came the most severe test her faith had yet endured: Her brother—Christian who had been praying for her for five years—died in an accident.

At first, prison officials refused to let Linda attend the funeral. They could not spare the guards. But correctional officers volunteered their own time to escort her to the funeral in nearby Newport News. Even in tragedy, she saw evidence of God's care.

Other inmates began to ask about the changes they saw in her. Although she knew God was changing her, the healing process was slow.

The root of Linda's drug dependency—low self-esteem—was not as quickly resolved as the addiction itself. Years of trying to earn love, yet not living up to others' ideals, were hard to erase. She needed the affirmation of people around her.

As Linda's parole date drew near, the churchgoers who led a Bible study at the women's prison reinforced her feelings of rejection. They only helped people in prison; she'd have to make it on her own in the "real world."

Once released, Linda joined a church where the members wanted only to preach at her and "lay hands" on her, self-righteously praying away her problems. No one ever said, "Want to go to lunch?"

Without Christian fellowship, the crisis of adjustment was overpowering. "You reap what you sow," says Linda, "and the harvest was coming in fast." The dealer she had lived with, and since married, walked out shortly after her return. It was worse than prison, because my last source of security was gone. I knew then I was alone," she says.

All alone in her apartment, Linda stared through tears at the dingy walls. Everything seemed distorted and far away. Her body numb, she staggered to the medicine cabinet—then to the refrigerator. "This is not worth it," she thought, downing several pills with a glass of wine.

When Linda awoke in a hospital, things were clearer. God's love—and God's love only—had seen her through. Thanking God for sparing her life, she told Him, "I have nowhere else to go but You."

Filled with new hope, Linda began attending a Richmond ex-offenders' Bible study at the home of Prison Fellowship volunteers John and Alexandra "Alex" Wickstead. The Wicksteads treated Linda—and all ex-offenders—like one of the family, and she thrived under their loving care.

John and Alex demonstrated a new concept to Linda: a husband and wife dedicated to glorifying God. "I had to learn about relationships all over again," says Linda. "They modeled a good marriage for me, teaching me how to have an argument and still love.''

Spending time with Alex, a woman equally at home serving tea or leading a Bible study in prison, taught Linda a self-esteem and gracefulness she had never known. Alex also gave Linda practical advice, coaching her in good nutrition. John counseled her with fatherly wisdom. Like her heavenly Father, they proved their love to her over and over again.

In response to the Wicksteads' love, Linda learned to love her parents. ''I learned to look at my parents with God's eyes,'' says Linda, ''and to accept them as He accepted me.''

During that time, Linda took an entry-level job with a large technical corporation and was promoted from clerk-typist to design technician. As she matured in her relationship with Christ and became confident in her job, her self-esteem blossomed. She was weaned from the insecurity that made her lean on people—especially men—rather than God.

It was at the Wicksteads' that Linda met Frank Bowman, the handsome, sandy-haired insurance salesman whom she eventually married. Frank, who led a weekly Bible study in a Richmond men's prison, was yet another sign of God's restoration.

''I needed every one of those seven years from the time I surrendered my life to God until He brought Frank to me,'' says Linda. ''God became my Resource, my Encourager, and my Husband. So when I met Frank, I didn't *need* him, but was able to *love* him.

''During the courtship,'' she continues, ''I kept saying, 'Lord, let us do it right—how it's supposed to be.' '' After two years of marriage, Linda knows her life is as it is supposed to be: lived in obedience to God.

As she and Frank look forward to the birth of their first child, Linda marvels again at God's restoration. As part of that restoration, she and Frank participate in nearby Prison Fellowship In-Prison Seminars, often laying the groundwork and recruiting volunteers.

Using her background and insights gained as a prisoner, Linda trains other Prison Fellowship volunteers. "I really enjoy providing vision for people. Sometimes they try to treat the surface symptoms; I've experienced the root problems."

Linda has learned the reality of 2 Corinthians 2:14, "[God] comforts us in all our troubles so that we can comfort those in any trouble with the comfort we ourselves have received from God."

Referring to the life she once knew, Linda says, "People who are hurting only know worldly ways to lick wounds. But no one can heal them like Jesus."

—*Alice Lawson Cox*

8

OMAR GONZALES

WHEN
THE GOOD LIFE
GIVES OUT

Cuban refugee Omar Gonzales came to the U.S. looking for freedom. He never suspected he'd end up serving time.

The squeeze was tight. On May 16, 1980, 250 refugees from Cuba crowded onto a shrimp boat made to hold 125—maximum. Like most of the other emigrants, 30-year-old Omar Gonzales had abandoned everything—family, friends, job—to chase the elusive dream of freedom.

The political refugee spent the night retching into the choppy sea, hoping, praying he'd make it to Key West. He'd tried to escape his homeland three times before. Omar knew the ache of defeat. But finally, shortly after dawn, he spotted pelicans on the horizon, then a beach. This was it.

As Omar walked down the gangplank, a uniformed immigration officer handed him a Coca-Cola—as if it were a prize or a symbol of the good life to follow.

That afternoon, Omar and other Marielitos (the 125,000 emigrants who left from Mariel harbor during the 60-day boat lift) sat under U.S. government tents, gorging themselves on hot dogs and potato chips. "It was a tremendous feeling of plenteousness," says the Cuban exile. "You could serve yourself as much as you wanted. In my country everything is strict, the food is rationed; it was really a shock."

A few days later, Omar boarded a government plane

bound for Fort Chaffee, Arkansas. While in flight, he employed his broken English to translate for the crew and passengers. He was happy to be of service in his new land.

After 45 days in the tent compound, he tracked down and convinced the one American he knew—a bachelor he'd met at a Hemingway fishing tournament—to sponsor him. No longer living under the threat of deportment, Omar moved to the Virginia suburbs of Washington, D.C.

Working as a laborer and part-time bartender, Omar soaked in the opulence of the new land. Having subsisted on three-fourths of a pound of meat every nine days and five pounds of rice per month (plus what he could get on the black market), he wandered supermarket aisles in amazement. How could he choose one brand of bread out of twenty?

It was all too much, too soon. "I went bizarre trying to replace twenty years of communism in one year," says Omar. "Having never been in a democracy, I didn't know how to handle myself."

He especially didn't know how to handle credit cards, the seductive tempters of the good life. They embodied the American dream, the ability to have anything he and his new wife wanted. Having established credit by purchasing two cars, he was courted by MasterCard, Diner's Club, and American Express. He took up their magical offers and charged away his life—enjoying a fancy stereo, expensive jewelry, and lavish vacations. With plastic wands he pursued his idea of freedom— the freedom to feel important.

"I was Mr. Rockefeller," he says. "American Express offered me a $15,000 credit line; it was incredible. When they send you a card like that, you have to use it."

But eventually, Omar's dream turned into a nightmare. He visited a fellow immigrant in early 1984, and, overcome with a debt of tens of thousands of dollars, asked how his friend afforded his luxurious lifestyle. The answer? Cocaine.

Convinced it was a harmless drug, Omar began selling

and using it. "I used to go to parties where they served marijuana and cocaine on silver plates. At one point I started believing drugs were legal because they were everywhere." As he became enmeshed in drug trafficking, however, Omar realized he was snared in a deadly trap. The people—and their white powder—were dangerous. "Something inside of me was saying, 'Get locked up and get out of this mess.'" When an undercover agent threw him to the ground and stuck a gun to his head, Omar was terrified, yet oddly relieved.

Six months after entering the drug world, Omar sat in a county jail staring at a Bible someone had handed him. He remembered his youthful days in the Roman Catholic church before Castro came to power and his teenage years handing out tracts for an underground church. "I didn't really know Jesus personally; I just liked the risk." More recently, he had lost his university teaching post and narrowly escaped imprisonment for telling one student he thought God had created the world.

Now, as a criminal with his back turned to God, he had been *given* the outlawed book. "It blew my mind away," says Omar. "I thought if you were a convict, drug dealer, you were of no worth. That Bible symbolized a love I had never experienced."

Feeling deserted by his wife, with no friends or family near, he was lonely. "God, I'm nothing," he said. "Nobody cares about me." A year later, in fall 1985, Omar attended a Prison Fellowship In-Prison Seminar (IPS) at the Virginia state prison where he was serving time. "I was drawn by the poster with people holding hands," he says. "I kept seeing those clasped hands, their unity." At the IPS, Omar met Prison Fellowship volunteer Jimmie Massie, a stockbroker turned farmer. As their friendship developed through Prison Fellowship Bible studies and visits, Omar became secure in God's love through His people. "In prison I felt guilty about how much damage I did to teenagers, businessmen—who knows?—but I took all that guilt to Christ and left it there."

Last December, Omar was paroled after serving three years in prison. He was given a change of clothes and $80. "I couldn't have made it without Jimmie, or someone with his love, concern and willingness to risk," says Omar. "He and other PF volunteers gave me capital and a place to live. They provided encouragement when I needed it most."

They also taught him to make—and stick to—a budget. His first two paychecks went toward debts that had been outstanding when he was jailed. The godly discipline Omar learned in prison and the relationship he developed with Jimmie helped him once he gained freedom. This time he could handle its responsibilities. "I learned in prison to trust God for everything, to put Christ first in everything."

Three months out of prison, Omar began teaching high-school equivalency classes to prisoners near Richmond. Although ex-prisoners are rarely allowed into prison so soon after release, Jimmie convinced the Department of Corrections (DOC) of Omar's skill and integrity. As one DOC official acknowledged, "Our business is trying to re-establish people in the community, to give them a chance to rebuild their lives. We ought to be right in it ourselves."

Omar was thrilled to be used as Christ's instrument, to bring love to a place of great need. "It was a dream come true to go back and let them know through my walk—not my talk—that Jesus remakes you, that you don't have to live in crime."

Omar also got part-time work at a hospital for drug addicts. Having been a prisoner of the state—and of drugs—he commands the respect of those still captive. "Today I'm able to say something I wasn't able to say before, that I am concerned and I *love* you. I see transfigured faces when I say that. Until Prison Fellowship, nobody ever confronted me and said, 'Omar, I love you.' "

As Omar now celebrates his eighth year in America, he

has a new understanding of the land of promise. "America is no longer America where I'm going to be rich," he says. "Today I enjoy people a lot more. And I would like God to use me to reflect His love to other people."

He also better understands liberty. Having lived under communism—where life was threatened—and capitalism—where the pursuit of happiness led to despair—Omar has found true liberty in Christ. "Freedom today," he says, "is the freedom of worship, the freedom of fellowship, and the freedom to express myself toward the One who created me. That's real freedom."

—Alice Lawson Cox

9

JIM BECKETT

A SUNDAY SCHOOL CLASS GOES TO PRISON

J im Beckett's mind raced. Why hadn't he noticed it before? He'd studied the Bible from Genesis to Revelation two or three times; he'd taught Sunday school for years. He must have read this verse—but never before had Matthew 25:43 seized his attention. He could almost hear Christ saying it: *I was sick and in prison, and you did not visit me.*

The successful 59-year-old businessman was not accustomed to surprises. As a Sunday school teacher, his time spent preparing each week's lesson had become routine: He'd sit at his desk, pray for guidance, open the Bible to the selected Scripture verses, and write down questions he would ask his adult Sunday school class at St. Peter's Episcopal Church.

But now Jim stared at the passage. It pierced his conscience. He shot up from his chair and began to pace. Why the powerful impact?

Things Jim hadn't thought of for years came to his mind—like unconnected pieces of a puzzle. His pastor had mentioned the verse; Jim recalled the name of a prison chaplain who regularly attended St. Peter's—Chaplain Ames. Surely he had referred to it, too; then there was the casual comment a member of his Sunday school class had made several years before. "I've been thinking," his friend had said, "we ought to visit guys in prison." At the time, Jim agreed: "Yeah, we ought to do something like that," but then the issue had been dropped.

Jim stopped pacing. The puzzle picture came together in his mind: The 15 to 20 members of his Sunday school class at St. Peter's could—should—be the "we" who visited prisoners.

"I felt my Bible study group had to have a focus," says Jim, now 61. "You just can't go to church Sunday after Sunday, meet and meet and meet . . . You must have an outreach—it should be something everyone can participate in." That outreach, he knew, would be visiting inmates.

Jim bounced the idea off his wife, Jane. She was immediately enthusiastic. "Even though I'd never known someone who'd been to prison, I like people," says Jane. "And I figured if we were allowed into prison, God would take care of us, and He would use us."

Jim called Ames, one of two chaplains at the nearby multi-level-security Federal Correctional Institution, Terminal Island. "How can we help you?" Jim asked.

Within the hour, Jim had all the information he needed. They would serve as volunteers for a forthcoming Prison Fellowship In-Prison Seminar. The thought pleased him: No longer would the Sunday school group be merely hearers of the Word; they would be doers as well.

The Terminal Island seminar focused on self-esteem. After each short teaching session, the participants broke into small groups for discussion. Jim and Jane joined one such group, personally getting to know about 10 inmates, including Steve Delman, the Christian "leader of the pack."

Steve, a tall, lanky man in his mid-thirties, had committed his life to Jesus Christ six months earlier. Jim and Jane didn't know why Steve was in prison; to them the past wasn't as important as the present—and the future. One thing was obvious, however: "Steve had been completely transformed by the Holy Spirit."

Jim came away from the seminar with a plan for future

ministry: The Sunday school class could hold a weekly communion service for Terminal Island inmates, followed by prayer and fellowship. Slowly, members of the Sunday school class began making friendships with inmates, as Jim was with Steve.

A short time later, Prison Fellowship sponsored another In-Prison Seminar at Terminal Island, which focused on biblical authority. "The message really hit home," says Jim, one of several members from St. Peter's at the seminar. Nearing retirement age, Jim felt nudged to spend even more time in ministry, and perhaps less time at Fibernetics—the once floundering fiber glass and plastics business he had bought nine years earlier and built into a prosperous company.

For several days after the seminar, biblical authority weighed on Jim's mind. While sitting in his office overlooking Fibernetics, Jim pondered the message: *In prison, you have to obey the rules,* he remembered hearing. *Sometimes we obey on the outside, but not on the inside—not in our hearts.*

He felt a pang of uneasiness in the thought: Am I holding back? Avoiding an answer, Jim gazed at the panoramic view in front of him.

His employees scurried back and forth, from one building to another. "I have a pretty good-sized company here," he heard himself say. Then he stopped short. In the silence that followed, Jim said, "No Lord, it's not mine; it's Yours."

"It came to me what I should do," Jim says. "It was time I let my son have control of the company." Jim's 33-year-old son, Chris, already owned half of the business, and was vice-president and general manager.

In mid-1985, Jim took his son to dinner and told him the news: Chris would become Fibernetics's president and chief executive officer.

"God has honored that decision in a fantastic way," Jim adds. With Chris in charge of Fibernetics, Jim was free to get involved more deeply in prison ministry. The weekly communion service became a Bible study, as members from St. Peter's began to share their Sunday school lessons with the inmates.

Every week, about 10 people—not always the same from week to week—belonging to the Sunday school class participate in the outreach. One couple didn't let their thirty-seventh wedding anniversary keep them from going. Another couple wanted to go one particular night, but apologized because the husband had to go to the hospital for cancer treatment instead.

Jim's encouraged not only with the group's dedication to the in-prison Bible study; they have begun to reach out to others as well. For example, each week a different member takes the Sunday school lesson to a housebound woman.

Meanwhile, after 17 years in prison, Steve Delman gained his release from Terminal Island. Jim wanted to help his close friend readjust to society. But how? His desire led him into an unexpected area of prison ministry: Aftercare.

The thought of hiring ex-offenders hadn't occurred to Jim: that is, until Steve was released. *Can we use these guys in the business?* Jim wondered.

When Jane said, "I think Steve would be good as a driver . . . Let's ask Chris to interview him," Jim's question was answered.

After a stay at a Long Beach halfway house, Steve was hired to work at a local chemical outlet. He and Jim had kept in touch regularly since his release, so it wasn't unusual for Jim to call Steve to chat. In one conversation Jim asked Steve if he would consider working for Fibernetics. "I want you to learn the business," he added.

"He didn't say, 'I want to give you a job,' " says Steve, "but 'I want you to learn the business.' " Steve recognized the tone of a father speaking to his son. Chris interviewed Steve for the position, and hired him soon after.

Over a year has passed since Steve joined Fibernetics. He is now the company's shipping and warehousing supervisor. "I thank God for the privilege of working here," adds Steve. "He's opened the door not only for me, but for others who come from a similar background."

Because of Steve's success at Fibernetics, Chris has hired other ex-offenders recommended by his parents or Steve. In fact, each person at the Terminal Island Bible study is a "potential employee," Jim says. Ernie Santa Cruz and Frank Granados, two of the some 75 employees at Fibernetics, are also former inmates.

Every Wednesday morning at 10:30, Jim meets with the three former inmates employed at Fibernetics. They talk about specific problems they are having adjusting to life after prison. And Jim offers godly advice for everyday living.

Along with the regular in-prison Bible study, the Becketts also find time to counsel ex-offenders and volunteer for other Prison Fellowship programs, such as In-Prison Seminars and Project Angel Tree. They received an 'outstanding volunteer service award' from Prison Fellowship in October 1986.

Since their initial involvement in prison ministry, Jim and Jane have moved to Rancho Palos Verdes. As Jim stands on the deck of their home, built on the side of a mountain, he looks into the distance. What he sees is representative of his new perspective: "Fibernetics is somewhere out there," he says as he points toward the horizon. Then he refers to places closer to home.

"From here we can see St. Peter's Episcopal Church," Jim says, pointing on the immediate left. After a pause, he turns to the right. "And over there, the green tower, is Terminal Island Prison.

"Going there each week is very natural for us," and he obviously speaks on behalf of his Sunday school class. "It doesn't take a lot of courage on our parts; it takes obedience. The Bible study at Terminal Island just followed out of obedience to Jesus' words in Matthew 25."

—Dean Ridings

10

BUD & SUE RICHMOND

HEALING A MARRIAGE WOUNDED BY CRIME

I need you, Bud." When the boss spoke, Bud Richmond listened. But this September 1984 appeal was not the usual Monday-morning money-talk between the president and vice-president of S. D. Cox Investments in Medford, Oregon.

He had a week to consider his boss's words, yet Bud was dazed. "So the books may not add up, but it's nothing we can't handle. There's no need to run—is there?" His concerns bounced off the boss.

A week later, when investigators from the Oregon State Securities Division arrived at the company's office for their scheduled appointment, Bud and his boss were on their way out of town.

In blind faith Bud, 33, followed the leader—even though it meant leaving Sue, his wife of 13 years, and their two boys, Jeremy and Brett. Why? He trusted and respected the man in the driver's seat—from the small town he'd grown up in, his friend since grade school.

Bud had joined S. D. Cox Investments three years earlier because he had craved what his friend possessed—a Mercedes-Benz for work, a Porsche for pleasure, a mansion on the hilltop; in short, money to burn. To Bud, money was the remedy and his boss held the prescription—which worked.

The last thing he wanted to do was run from his lucrative job. But as he stared at his boss in the seat next to him, Bud realized that there was no turning back; the decision had already been made.

They drove south from Medford to San Francisco. On the way Bud noticed a book in his boss's loosely packed luggage and examined its black and yellow cover: *Born Again*.

"Where'd this come from?" Bud asked.

"An attorney friend who knows the author, Chuck Colson."

Now having a lot of time on his hands, Bud thumbed through the pages. Chapter 1 caught his eyes: "Something Wrong."

To Bud the story was familiar: A man puts his trust in another man's hands and not in God's. As Bud read about Colson's search for Jesus Christ, his own search surfaced in his consciousness.

"I wanted the same thing," recalls Bud. "I wanted to take this old life and bury it." But for a while Bud stayed loyal to his boss, "running" farther west, to Hawaii, where the two men began a scrap gold and silver business. Bud started attending church. And before long, he asked Jesus to give him the new life Colson had found. Though he wasn't ready to go home, he called Sue and told her of his new commitment. Then he urged her to get a copy of *Born Again* to see what it was all about.

Like Bud, Sue empathized with Colson. She wanted to know more about the One who could change a life so radically, but she didn't know how to go about it. Gathering her courage, she called upon a minister she'd known and bared her soul.

"I told him how I was feeling," she says. "But he didn't help. He didn't tell me about a relationship with Jesus Christ . . . So I just became more frustrated."

Meanwhile, Sue did everything she could to keep herself and her family together. Yet no matter how determined, she began to sink under the weight of Bud's absence. Relentless questions from family and friends forced her to retreat into her home—even into her bedroom—where the accusations echoed in the darkness.

"Where's Bud?" *I don't know.* "Why'd he desert you?" *He didn't desert me.* "Will he ever come back?" *He'll be back.* "Will he go to prison?" *I don't know.* Even the few people who stuck by her seemed to ask: "Aren't you going to file for divorce?" *No.*

Sue got through the Christmas holidays by pouring bourbon into her hot tea. In the dead of winter, she found herself putting things in order, making plans, revising her will—subtly preparing to take her own life. "I just wanted to quit," she recalls. "I didn't want to hurt anymore."

About that time Bud called with a suggestion: "Try Applegate Christian Fellowship," a local church. Sue's voice was low, weary. She was tired of the games—running from phone booth to phone booth to talk with her husband, making excuses for his absence.

"If you're really a Christian, if you really care," she said, "why aren't you here?" Bud sidestepped the question, but insisted she try the church.

A few days later a friend called to say she, too, was in the land of the deserted: Her husband had just left her for another woman. "What are you going to do?" Sue asked.

To Sue's surprise, she said, "I'm going to church . . . Applegate Christian Fellowship. Do you want to come?" The next night the two sat together; on Sunday Sue accepted Jesus Christ.

In July 1985, Bud finally realized that following Jesus meant going back to Medford to face the music—even though he knew the tune wouldn't be a cheerful one.

"I knew the company was in arrears, but I thought it was

just $500,000 or so, not a lot for a business," says Bud. "Little by little, the longer I was out [on the run], the more I found out, and the more conviction I was under to come back and try to take care of things." And so he returned—to an exasperated yet glad family—and turned himself in.

Bail set at $800,000 assured the state that their prize catch would not get away. Bud's lawyer urged him to agree to a "lenient" plea bargain deal—one "Class A" felony for racketeering instead of four "Class C" felonies—and a naive Bud consented. To everyone's shock, the judge gave him a 15-year prison sentence. "You'll have to pay restitution, too."

Once he was sitting in the Oregon State Penitentiary, Bud studied his Bible, went to chapel, and helped lead several fellow prisoners to Christ. But, considering his long sentence and painful past, Bud saw no hope for his marriage. When he was transferred to OSP's farm annex, Bud filed for divorce.

But the words from another Chuck Colson book he'd read on the run, *Loving God*, wouldn't let him rest: To love God is to believe, to repent, to follow, to obey . . .

"Loving God means *obeying* God," says Bud. "I knew that asking for a divorce wasn't being obedient. Three days before the divorce was to be final, I, like the Prodigal Son, finally came to myself: I'd been disobedient to God."

Bud called Sue and begged her not to sign the divorce papers. He then started sending love notes and wooing Sue as he had in high school—winning her over. In September 1986 Sue and the boys moved close to the prison so they could regularly visit Bud. Within days she found a house and a job as an office worker.

As an inmate, Bud started working as a data processor for Lou Lewandowski, a Christian corrections manager hired by the release center to manage its computer operation. Lou quickly became a friend. In an effort to bring prisoners' families together for worship, Lou and Bud worked with the head of the release center to organize a program that allows some inmates to be escorted to Sunday evening services outside the facility at local Morning Star Christian Church.

Today, nearly a year after his early release, Bud still works for Lou as a full-time data processor for the release center. And the Richmond family still attends Morning Star, which now sponsors several Prison Fellowship programs.

Bud leads the Philemon Fellowship group for ex-prisoners that gathers in the Richmond living room every Thursday night. And Sue spends that evening at the church leading a Spouse Fellowship group, attended primarily by wives of current and former inmates.

Bud tells the small, committed group that meets in his home about tying their problems to the Cross—"just the way the priests tied the rams down when they sacrificed them in the Old Testament," he says. "Don't pick them back up again. Tie them to the Cross and walk away."

The group nods as Bud speaks from experience. "Trouble with your wife? Jealous? Frustrated?" As if he were a "broken record," Bud points them to the Cross. It's how Bud and Sue deal with their problems, including the potentially devastating one that recently hit them: When Bud went to sign his parole papers, he discovered the state's order to pay restitution for the entire loss at S. D. Cox Investments, Incorporated, exceeding $3 million.

"The Lord took me through my incarceration. He restored my marriage. He can handle this restitution too. Nothing is too big for Him," testifies Bud. Today, a large amount of the Richmonds' monthly income goes toward the restitution.

Sue's support group operates in much the same way, and the problems are similar.

"I'm so angry at my husband," one woman says through tears. "It's so difficult to forgive!"

"We must let Christ—not our feelings—rule our lives," responds a sympathetic Sue. "We can't leave open little windows for the Enemy to enter through to destroy us." Pats of agreement, arms of support, tears of love, and there is strength for the road ahead.

"If we're instrumental in nothing else than to help one marriage make it," says Bud, "then Glory to God, because that's what it's about." Robert and Janie are one couple struggling to hold it together, and finding encouragement in the support groups.

In fact, Robert—an ex-prisoner Bud first met at the release center—challenged Bud in the first place to start the Philemon Fellowship. "Janie comes home from Sue's group and *she's nice,*" Robert had said. "She spends two hours there, sharing and praying. She comes home so nice it makes me mad. I want the same thing, so we'll both be okay."

Bud says Robert and Janie are now in the process of "molding themselves back together as husband and wife," and healing. "And that's a witness to their kids," says Bud, "and it's a witness to other couples with broken relationships."

Bud and Sue remain "on call" at all times if somebody in one of their groups needs help. The Richmonds also have encouragers—people like Mark Hubbell, Prison Fellowship's local area director, and his wife, Deb.

In both support groups, especially when discussing following Jesus Christ and none other, Bud and Sue's testimony offers hope. "Our walk speaks louder than our talk," says Bud. "I was obedient when I decided to return home. I said, 'Jesus, make my life shine for You.' That's what people saw."

Their testimony is this: Jesus does restore marriages—no matter what you've gone through and no matter what you're going through. And the key to it is following Jesus Christ.

—*Dean Ridings*

11

MEL GOEBEL

AN EX·PRISONER LAYS HIS FAITH ON THE LINE

Omaha, Nebraska, February, 1971. "The court finds Melvin R. Goebel guilty on one count of burglary. He is sentenced to two to five years of hard labor at the Nebraska State Penitentiary."

T wo years later, 22-year-old Mel Goebel sat in the asphalt yard of Lincoln Correctional Center (LCC). The blue sky and warm, spring air reminded him of his former freedom. He stared at concrete walls and razor wire, thinking of ways to smuggle in pot, the drug that had helped him drift through this incarceration. Maybe his girlfriend would bring some on her next visit. His thoughts were distracted when a bus full of new prisoners—mostly uninitiated kids—arrived and started to unload.

Mel's blue eyes focused on a guy in a khaki jacket with black magic-marker lettering on the back: "Smile, Jesus is your friend."

Is that guy nuts? he thought. *The prisoners are going to tear him apart.*

Mel sauntered up to the kid and pulled him aside. "Tell me about this Jesus." There was a sneer in his voice. "I've never seen any love in people."

The new guy was silent for a moment, then he said, "Christ will give you peace of mind. He'll give you direction and overflow your life with joy and happiness."

Mel didn't have an answer, but later that night he pondered the young man's words. He remembered the Jesus of his childhood. He recalled getting dressed for mass and reciting prayers by rote, then coming home to a house without love. *Could this Jesus be real?*

The question wouldn't leave. After a few days he sought out Fred, the khaki-jacketed prisoner. "What about the suffering in the world?" he asked. "How come I've had to go through all this pain?"

"It's a walk of faith," Fred replied, opening his Bible. "You have to read the Holy Scriptures and come to grips with these questions yourself." Mel returned to his cell to think; later he borrowed a Bible from the chapel, and the words he read—of love and forgiveness—penetrated deep.

One day, Mel returned from work duty early. He knelt in the cell's curtained toilet area—tears rolling down his cheek—and confessed his sin. That day, he found God's forgiveness—and the peace he'd been looking for.

Being a Christian changed Mel's outlook on prison. Before, he had constantly thought about getting out. Now, he learned to be content. He viewed prison as a monastery where he could study the Bible, form close friendships, and practice his Christianity.

News of his conversion spread quickly: One of the friends with whom Mel used to get high was in solitary confinement when Mel accepted the Lord. When Rick returned to the general population, he sought out Mel. Rick was angry that he had lost a friend, and he doubted Mel's sincerity.

Mel told Rick how Jesus had brought him forgiveness, and showed him passages in the Bible. That afternoon, standing in the yard, Rick committed his life to the Lord. Later he became a strong leader in the prison church.

About a year later, an 18-year-old inmate named Rocky came to Mel's cell. He, too, had heard about Mel's conversion. With tears in his eyes, the boy explained his story: When he had first come to prison he had accepted a carton of pot and some cigarettes from older inmates. Now the "Goon Squad" wanted to collect payment in homosexual "favors."

Not sure what to do, Mel and some other Christians scraped together their change and bought a carton of cigarettes at the commissary. Then Mel walked alone to the gym where the inmates—his old gang—waited. Right away, he spotted Eric, the tall, muscled black man who had once been his leader.

"It was the first time my faith was on the line," Mel says. "When I saw those four guys standing there, I realized that, since coming to Christ, I'd forgotten the prison code of toughness."

He walked to the back of the gym and held out the cigarettes. "Here's the carton Rocky owes you," he said. "I never collected the two cartons of pot you owed me, so the debt is cancelled."

Eric stepped forward. "Who do you think you are, telling us what to do?"

Mel's heart beat hard, but he stood his ground. "Because of Christ, Rocky's my brother," he said his voice shaking. "I have to help him." Expecting to be jumped, Mel turned and walked away. But no one followed.

Back in the yard, Mel told two other Christian inmates what had happened. As they talked, one of them looked up and saw Eric walking toward them. Seven or eight big guys surrounded him, swearing and encouraging him to beat up Mel.

The three Christians exchanged looks; what would Jesus have them do? "The servant is not greater than the Master," one of them said. Jesus has been bruised and battered. If people had persecuted Him, they would persecute His followers, too.

Mel says, "We were prepared to take a beating for the Lord. After four years in prison, I knew people who would fight for me, but we decided against it. Even though I was afraid, I knew the Lord was with me."

When Eric was face to face with Mel, he scowled. "I don't

think I like what you did down there." He moved closer.

Mel took a deep breath and looked his old leader in the eyes. "Eric, if you were being threatened I would do the same thing for you."

The gang leader turned and walked away; he hadn't seen that kind of love before. Slowly, the others followed.

"That day," says Mel, "I learned that 1 John 4:4 holds true: 'Greater is he that is in you, than he that is in the world.' I also learned the importance of warning new inmates about prison traps." Subsequently, Mel and his brothers greeted the weekly bus loads of inmates and told them about the Christian community at LCC.

When Mel was released in 1976, he left the company of one Christian fellowship, but walked into the arms of a supportive group in Omaha. Dallen Peterson, a businessman who had led Bible studies at LCC for two years, helped Mel get a job. Dallen and his wife, Glennis, also opened their home to Mel. During his first year out, Mel visited them almost daily. They provided the loving family and church life he had never known.

And at Calvary Lutheran Church, Mel met Jane Danitschek, whom he married in 1979. Shortly after their wedding, Jane's father gave Mel a copy of *Jubilee*. Mel was impressed with what he saw. He contacted Prison Fellowship and attended a Washington Discipleship Seminar, where they saw evidence of his mature faith. A few months later, he joined Prison Fellowship's staff as a state director. His compassion for people helped him nurture both volunteers and inmates.

In 1983, after helping Prison Fellowship get started in Colorado, Mel returned to Omaha to pursue a college degree. This was a big step for someone who had dropped out of eleventh grade because of a prison sentence. Prison Fellowship kept Mel on staff part time, so he continued to work with prisoners in Omaha.

One of Mel's greatest accomplishments was to start a

Philemon (ex-offender) Fellowship. "With Philemon," says Mel, "Prison Fellowship has come full circle by providing support on the outside—as well as the inside—of prisons."

Mel, too, has come full circle. Last December he stood in the Nebraska capitol and appealed for a state pardon. He wanted his crime erased from the records so he could enjoy the full rights of a citizen. He explained that he had "paid his dues," then devoted his life to helping others.

As he awaited the verdict, Mel shifted in his seat. At last, the governor arose and announce that Mel would receive a full pardon. The slate was washed cleaned. "Forgiveness is instant with God," says Mel, "but with society it takes much longer."

Referring to the hearing, Mel says, "It reminded me that someday we all are going to face God. I didn't know if the state would pardon me, but I do know God has forgiven my sins. If I was that nervous in a secular courtroom, how will people who are not confident of Jesus' forgiveness feel before the throne of God? Because I know that He can forgive, I need to tell others. For me, that calling is in prison."

—*Alice Lawson Cox*

12

WILLIE RIOS

MY STRUGGLE TO GO STRAIGHT

I thought I'd been through the worst—shooting drugs, sleeping on rooftops, in trucks, wherever the night caught me. I'd done time in every prison or jail in New York City. But when, out of desperation, I entered Manhattan's men's shelter, I lost whatever dignity I had left.

I used to look down on alcoholics clinging to their wine bottles. Now I'd become one of them, walking the Bowery, talking to myself, and making no sense. Scaring people in the street away from me.

I thought, *I'm going back to shooting drugs; it's more sophisticated than being an alcoholic.* I started ripping off cars to afford the cocaine but, again, the cycle of drugs and money got to be too much. I went back to the alcohol—asking for nickels and dimes on the corner.

One night, I was thinking about how to get high again. Then suddenly it was like my mind was invaded: *Come out. I want you now,* someone seemed to say. *Get your life together and follow me.* I'd gone to church when I was a kid; I knew I was having a spiritual experience.

With the little faith that I had, I walked to Manhattan General Hospital. I stood outside all night smoking cigarettes. When they opened the doors the next morning, I was still waiting. I was the first one admitted for detox—to kick the alcohol and the heroin.

From the hospital I went to a resident drug program. Now I had to find out who God was. I found a Bible left in the dorm and began reading it. At night I would hallucinate. I'd wake up cursing and yelling, scaring the other guys living there.

I dreaded going to sleep and being attacked by dreams from my past. When they came I'd cry out to the Lord—not knowing (for sure) that there was a God listening. I still had shakes from the alcohol. I wanted to get high. The Lord hadn't yet taken the desire away.

I was tempted to go back, to get out from under the pressure and the agony of trying to get my life together. Many times before, when I'd come out of jail, I'd had the desire to go straight. But, because I'd failed so many times, I'd say, "Hey, sooner or later I'm going to shoot dope anyway. I might as well do it now."

As soon as I was allowed out of the drug center on passes I went looking for a church. There were churches on every other block, but I couldn't find one that felt right. Then a sister of one of the guys in the program invited me to her church—Brooklyn Tabernacle.

When I walked into that church lobby in September 1981, the first guy I saw was Ray Robles, a friend from my old Williamsburg neighborhood in Brooklyn. I was excited to see somebody I knew, just like when you walk into prison and you see one of the home boys. You don't feel so alone. He was as happy to see me, and we hugged each other. He said, "Wow, Willie, we had heard you were dead. We actually thought you were dead." He said, "Guess what? Ace is here." Ace used to be the president of our old gang. He got Ace out of choir practice. When Ace saw me he yelled and hugged me. To see these guys straight was my first real joy since seeking the Lord. We had a reunion right there in the church lobby.

I went back to the drug program feeling so good. I said,

"Ya know, I think this is it. I went back the following Sunday . . . I kept going back. But I didn't commit myself to the church or the Lord yet. *If I'm going to give my heart to Jesus*, I thought, *I want to make sure I'm doing it right. I've been gaming all my life—I don't want to game with this.* So I would look at how the pastor dressed, what kind of rings he had on, what kind of car he got into, because I didn't want to be hustled.

Then, after three or four months, I made my commitment to the Lord. The pastor was preaching on sins of the past, how they could hold you back, how they can be the worst thing that the Enemy can use against you. I knew he was right. I was ready to let go. I cried in that service.

I look back now and I see how long God had been working in my life. So many times I took overdoses . . . and would wake up 10, 12 hours later, when I should have been dead. Once, in a fight, I was shot in the head but the bullet missed my brain. All these things weren't coincidence.

I joined the church's street ministry. I would sing in the choir, give my testimony . . . how the Lord brought me from the rat holes of life. Sometimes I got so excited that I'd wish I could just grab them and make them see that what I had was real.

As I learned more about grace and the power of Jesus' blood and freedom in Christ, I'd go to churches and speak or counsel people with drug problems. Sometimes, when the church choir went into a prison, I'd give my testimony. Every time I spoke in one of those jails I'd be surrounded by inmates who knew I understood and that I cared. I could give them hope because I'd been there—on the streets, in the gangs.

Working in the streets, I'd see guys so high on dope that they really couldn't see they had a problem. Guys in prison can see that their lives have gone wrong. Their feelings of self-doubt are near the surface. They're looking for help.

So, in October 1986, I began going into three New York City jails regularly, and I also helped with Spanish services in prisons upstate. Even when I didn't give my testimony, I knew it helped the inmates to see another brother praising God.

Last October, Lefty Diaz, a friend of mine in the church, and I decided to start our own prison ministry. But we didn't know how to get started. Then our pastor told us about Ron Jacobs, the Prison Fellowship New York City area director. We went to see him at Prison Fellowship's office in lower Manhattan. What Ron told us about Prison Fellowship helped us to see that we didn't have to reinvent the wheel.

Prison Fellowship opens up prison doors churches can't open on their own. The literature they have is great. If we want to participate in an In-Prison Seminar, all the church has to do is provide the volunteers to make the program work.

Last Christmas I coordinated Prison Fellowship's Angel Tree program at Brooklyn Tabernacle. Then Ron asked me to be the PF volunteer coordinator for all New York City, supervising volunteer groups for In-Prison Seminars, Project Angel Tree, and family ministry. I feel a burden for the guys in prison bound by sin.

Two years ago, my older brother, who was in prison for murder, got AIDS. Another brother, Angelo, who's a pastor, and I finally got him transferred to a hospital last March. He was there only a few weeks before he died. I would tell him, "You can't save your *life*. But you can still save your soul."

But he was one who didn't even believe in the electric light bulb. I told him, "Bro, you've seen me with lice on me. You've seen me with dried defecation in my pants. Look at me now, man. Tell me there's no God." He finally understood.

In his last days he would want us to sing Christian songs and pray with him. When we would sing, "If you love my Jesus raise your hands," he would move his hand and pray. He was at peace. That's the freedom I feel burdened to take into prison.

—by Willie Rios as told to David Singer

In February of 1988, just after the above story was published, first Willie, then Debbie, were hospitalized with pneumonia. Both were diagnosed to have AIDS, which Willie had contracted at least seven years earlier from contaminated needles.

Willie and Debbie recovered from this initial bout with pneumonia in time for Willie to attend Prison Fellowship's In-Prison Seminar leadership training in June of 1988. The training further stimulated Willie's urgent desire to share Christ, yet he also continued to agonize over the guilt, pain, and disease he had brought to his marriage. A few weeks later Willie was again hospitalized.

On Saturday, September 10, 1988, Willie died. The following Tuesday 2,000 of his Christian family at Brooklyn Tabernacle celebrated his union with the Lord. His older brother Angelo Rios, now a pastor in the Bronx, read a farewell Willie had prepared. Willie began, ''I would like to express to all my brothers and sisters in the Lord to get involved in the Great Commission.''

Debbie also shared about her struggles and eventual peace. ''Even in the hospital Willie brought glory to God ministering to other people. Through Willie's fire and urgency God showed me how real the Great Commission is. In the final weeks I would say, 'God, You are able. You took Willie from the pit of hell . . . You won't let him die. His ministry is not finished yet.' Even though God showed me that the miracle was Willie's salvation, I clung on for a new miracle. I wanted Willie to be with me.'' And then God did another miracle. ''When I finally let the Lord have Willie, he stopped breathing, and I heard God say, 'Well done, my good and faithful servant.' ''

13

CHARLES COLSON

CRIME AND REDEMPTIVE PUNISHMENT

As a Christian, I most certainly believe in punishment. Biblical justice demands that individuals be held accountable. Throughout the history of ancient Israel, to break God's law was to invite swift, specific, and certain punishment. When a law was broken the resulting imbalance could be righted only when the transgressor was punished, and thus made to "pay" for his wrong.

Though modern sociologists take offense at this elemental concept of retribution, it is essential.

C. S. Lewis summed this up in "The Humanitarian Theory of Punishment," an essay assailing the view that lawbreakers should be "cured" or "treated" rather than punished: "To be punished, however severely, because we have deserved it, because we 'ought to have known better,' is to be treated as a human person made in God's image." In this sense, punishment is not only just, it is often redemptive—to the offender, the victim, and society at large.

This is why the distinction between prison and punishment is so crucial. Prisons, though necessary to confine violent offenders, can hardly be considered redemptive.

And while punishment is clearly biblical, American penal philosophy is not based on the biblical principle of just desserts that Lewis cited; it is founded on a humanistic view that crime is an illness to be cured.

The pattern for American prisons was established two centuries ago when well-meaning Quakers converted a Philadelphia jail into a facility where offenders were confined in order to repent and be rehabilitated.

Though a number of those early "penitents" simply went mad, the idea caught on and flourished. Soothed by the comforting illusion that these miscreants were in reality being "treated," the public conscience could ignore the harsh conditions of their confinement. Thus such places came to be called, not prisons, but *penitent*iaries, *reform*atories, and *correct*ional institutions.

This illusion was reinforced in the twentieth century when a school of liberal sociologists argued that crime was not the individual's fault, but society's. Societal failures like poverty, racism, and unemployment were to blame.

If the criminal was but a victim of the system, prisons were therefore places for him or her to be vocationally trained, "socialized," and educated. Society, which had caused the disease of crime, would now cure it—and so ever-increasing thousands were packed into institutions as wards of the state.

Thus two centuries of the "humanitarian tradition" left America with more than one half million of its citizens incarcerated—the third largest per capita prison population in the world. But these prisons proved themselves not places of rehabilitation, but breeding grounds for further crime.

Crime is the result of morally responsible people making wrong moral decisions, for which they must be held accountable. The just and necessary response to such behavior is redemptive punishment. But let's not kid ourselves any longer. Prison isn't to cure the individual. It's to lock him or her up.

It is crucial to expose the widespread illusion about punishment and prisons in America today. We have a national policy which stuffs our facilities with humanity, half of them nonviolent, and gives them nothing meaningful to do.

The Problem of Overcrowding

A few years ago, a research psychologist undertook the project of creating utopia on earth. Dr. John Calhoon of the National Institute of Mental Health constructed 16-room apartment units, in which residents would have regular meals, social opportunities, and a complete security system.

The 160 occupants were mice. But Calhoon believed his experiment would provide valuable insights into human behavior. If that's the case, what happened in "paradise" raises startling questions.

The mice settled into the good life, and they were prolific: 500 mice in the first litter. The young mice, quickly crowded out, huddled together, motionless but for occasional outbursts of violence. As they became more congested, many withdrew to simply eat, drink, and sleep. Reproduction ceased. Most frightening of all, their passive/aggressive behavior seemed irreversible. After five years of abundant food and water, protection from predators, disease, and mousetraps, the entire mouse community had died—simply crowded to death.

While the Calhoon experiments were intended to warn of the dangers of crowded ghettos, they provide an apt parable for America's prisons.

The prison population is increasing 10 times faster than the general population. It grew 113 percent between 1975 and 1985. In 1975 various levels of government in the U.S. spent $1.5 billion on corrections. In 1983 that figure had increased seven times. But as new prisons open, they are jammed beyond capacity almost overnight.

Tragically, there is no relief in sight. The state inmate population was expected to rise by 35 percent between 1984 and 1990. The cost of building new prisons, at $50,000 to $80,000 per bed, endangers many state budgets.

But these shocking statistics fail to capture the depth of

human devastation. I see the effects of overcrowding firsthand in almost every prison I visit. In the most notorious cellblock of an ancient midwestern prison there were double bunks in each six- by nine-foot cell. Some nights, a third inmate was made to sleep under the bottom bunk on the grimy concrete floor. Like Dr. Calhoon's mice, the longtimers seemed withdrawn, sullen, passive.

As I walked through this prison, I came to a cell with only one bunk. A grinning, younger inmate thrust his hand through the bars to shake mine. "How come you're here by yourself?" I asked.

Still grinning, he replied without hesitation: "Because I'd kill anybody they'd put in here."

The prison authorities believed him; so did I. Across the nation, most of the bloody riots of the last 15 years have been attributed directly to overcrowded conditions.

And the evidence is, as Dr. Calhoon suggested, that psychological damage from overcrowding is permanent. According to the FBI, 74 percent of those released from prison are rearrested within four years. On the outside, prisoners who are violent and aggressive continue that behavior; those who have withdrawn are just as helpless.

What is being done? Some states are blindly spending billions for new prisons. That's good news for the architects and builders who are generous contributors to the campaigns of local politicians. But it's bad news for the public.

The Problem of Idle Hours

In 1985 newspapers were full of reports of prison disturbances. Governor after governor appointed an investigative panel, which blamed everything on overcrowding, poor facilities, or mismanagement.

But during a visit to the site of two riots, I discovered an atypical prison, in that it was not overcrowded; the facilities were excellent and the staff well-trained. But for the fences, the institution could have been mistaken for a college campus. Yet inmates had beaten out a cement wall with their bare fists. Why?

The warden had no explanation. "But," he said, "of course we have no work here—only 100 jobs for 800 men. We make work."

"Make work." On the flight back to Washington, I couldn't forget those words—nor the devastated cellblock. In his offhand remark, the warden may very well have provided another key to the unrest.

The nation is indebted to Chief Justice Burger, who crusaded for more inmate jobs. He was on the right track.

Those who argue for prison jobs usually do so on the grounds that they are important for rehabilitation: Offenders need vocational skills when they get out.

That's true enough. But there's a more crucial theological reason, one that explains why our prisons drive men to despair. In the world around us, we can readily see order, harmony, and purpose; this is powerful evidence for the existence of a personal, orderly, and purposeful Creator.

Like the universe, mankind is created by God—in His very image. We are imbued with the same sense of purpose evident in our Creator. This affects not only our perception of life, but our practical, everyday relationships, recreation—and work.

The great Russian novelist, Feodor Dostoevsky, imprisoned for 10 years during a period of czarist repression, wrote, "If one wanted to crush, to annihilate a man utterly, to inflict on him the most terrible of punishments . . . one need only give him work of an absolutely, completely useless and irrational character."

Eugene Heimler, a Holocaust survivor, wrote of an experiment in which Jews who had been working in a prison factory were suddenly ordered to move sand from one end of their camp to another—back and forth, over a period of weeks.

Many prisoners, who had been able to cling to life even

while working for their hated captors, went berserk and were shot by guards. Others threw themselves into the electrified wire fence. Punishment? Yes. Biblical justice demands it. And prisons are necessary to separate dangerous offenders from society. But confining nondangerous men and women with nothing to do, driving them to the brink of their sanity? No.

There's an Alternative

Fortunately, some states are considering alternative punishments—not prison—for nonviolent offenders.

Florida, for example, where Prison Fellowship worked with lawmakers who faced facts, adopted model legislation in 1983 utilizing restitution, expanded probation, and early release programs methods of redemptive punishment. In the first three years, the corrections budget increased by only $60 million instead of the projected $300 million—and the crime rate dropped.

We need such courageous action from lawmakers in every state. Redemptive punishments may include, as the Bible prescribes, restitution or community service, stiff fines, loss of rights. Biblical righteousness demands a system of punishment that is swift, certain, and just. But that doesn't always mean prison.

—*Charles W. Colson*

NOTES

The stories in this book were taken from Prison Fellowship's newsletter, *Jubilee,* as listed below:

ABOUT PRISON FELLOWSHIP

Prison Fellowship is an interdenominational ministry to prisoners, ex-prisoners, and their families, founded in 1976 by Charles W. Colson. After serving seven months in prison for a Watergate-related offense, Colson devoted his life to working with prisoners.

In 1976 he started Prison Fellowship with two staff members and three volunteers. Since that time Prison Fellowship has grown phenomenally: 150 employees and 20,000 volunteers work in 48 U.S. states. And Prison Fellowship International has involvement with prison ministry groups in over 60 countries around the world.

Prison Fellowship believes that the first and most important step in true rehabilitation is a spiritual one—when an inmate consciously turns away from the old life to new life in Jesus Christ.

But that turning point is only the beginning. Inmates need teaching, guidance, encouragement, as well as practical-life skills. They need role models to help them see how to become respectable citizens who contribute to society. Prison Fellowship has developed a number of programs to help accomplish these goals. They include:

In-Prison Seminars

Three to five days of evangelistic and discipleship meetings in prison.

Bible Studies

Small-group weekly Bible studies, led by Prison Fellowship volunteers, follow In-Prison Seminars.

Ex-Prisoner Groups

Called Philemon Fellowships, these groups provide practical support for ex-prisoners.

Aftercare

Helps inmates to stay out of prison and get involved in a local church.

Angel Tree

Project that provides Christmas gifts to the children of inmates.

Family Ministry

Marriage Seminars, family counseling, training for spouses and children.

Community Service Projects

Where nonviolent offenders participate in community work projects that benefit society.

To continue this important ministry, we need your help. If you would like to become a volunteer or financial supporter of Prison Fellowship, please complete and mail the form on the following page today.

Thank you!

You Can Make a Difference

If you've been stirred by what you've read in this book, and you'd like to help Prison Fellowship bring the life-changing Gospel message to inmates across America, and to be a demonstration of the Gospel in action, please take a moment to complete and return the response below.

☐ Yes, I want to help Prison Fellowship win inmates to Christ and work to help solve America's prison crisis.

Enclosed is my gift of:
☐ $25   ☐ $35   ☐ $50   ☐ Other $ _____

☐ Please send me more information about becoming a Prison Fellowship volunteer.

_____
Name

_____
Address

_____
City, State, Zip

Thank you for caring. You will receive a tax-deductible receipt. Please return this form to:

Prison Fellowship Ministries
P.O. Box 17500
Washington, DC 20041–0500   9PR0100

Inspiring Best-Selling Books
by Chuck Colson

Born Again—The account of a conversion that startled the country and launched a ministry.
Paperback, BKAB0, **$3.95**

Loving God—A combination of dramatic storytelling and insightful exposition that explores the heights and depths involved in following Jesus Christ.
Paperback (with study guide), BKAK0, **$8.95**

Kingdoms in Conflict—A keen analysis of the conflicts between church and state in history, with illustrations of Christians who made a difference.
Hardback, BKBU0, Reg. $15.95, Available for **$12.95**

A New Perspective on Criminal Justice

Crime and Its Victims, Daniel Van Ness. A scriptural view of crime and punishment as it affects victims, prisoners, and the public.   Paperback, BKBL0, **$7.95**

- -

Please send me, postage-paid, the following books:

_____

I am enclosing a check in the amount of $ _____.
Virginia residents please include 4½% sales tax.

_____
Name

_____
Street Address

_____
City/State/Zip

Please mail this form to:

Fellowship Communications
P.O. Box 17152
Washington, DC 20041–0152

9FCBK01

You Can Make a Difference

If you've been stirred by what you've read in this book, and you'd like to help Prison Fellowship bring the life-changing Gospel message to inmates across America, and to be a demonstration of the Gospel in action, please take a moment to complete and return the response below.

☐ Yes, I want to help Prison Fellowship win inmates to Christ and work to help solve America's prison crisis.

Enclosed is my gift of:
☐ $25 ☐ $35 ☐ $50 ☐ Other $ _____

☐ Please send me more information about becoming a Prison Fellowship volunteer.

_____
Name

_____
Address

_____
City, State, Zip

Thank you for caring. You will receive a tax-deductible receipt. Please return this form to:

Prison Fellowship Ministries
P.O. Box 17500
Washington, DC 20041–0500

Inspiring Best-Selling Books
by Chuck Colson

Born Again—The account of a conversion that startled the country and launched a ministry.
Paperback, BKAB0, **$3.95**

Loving God—A combination of dramatic storytelling and insightful exposition that explores the heights and depths involved in following Jesus Christ.
Paperback (with study guide), BKAK0, **$8.95**

Kingdoms in Conflict—A keen analysis of the conflicts between church and state in history, with illustrations of Christians who made a difference.
Hardback, BKBU0, Reg. $15.95, Available for **$12.95**

A New Perspective on Criminal Justice

Crime and Its Victims, Daniel Van Ness. A scriptural view of crime and punishment as it affects victims, prisoners, and the public. Paperback, BKBL0, **$7.95**

- -

Please send me, postage-paid, the following books:

_____

I am enclosing a check in the amount of $ _____.
Virginia residents please include 4½% sales tax.

_____
Name

_____
Street Address

_____
City/State/Zip

Please mail this form to:

Fellowship Communications
P.O. Box 17152
Washington, DC 20041–0152